WHAT HAPPENS WHEN
Someone I love can't get better

SARA OLSHER with JENNI ROGERS, MS, CCLS, CTRS

Hi! My name is **Mia!**

And this is **Stuart.**

Stuart is very curious, and sometimes he feels a little worried when he doesn't understand something.

Stuart wants to know...
Why do some people's bodies stop working right?
And what if they can't get better?

Bodies are really, really **COOL!**
And what we can *see* is only
part of what makes bodies so cool.

Inside, there are lots of different body parts,
and each one has an important job.
These jobs give the body everything it needs,
like oxygen to breathe, energy to play, and so much more.

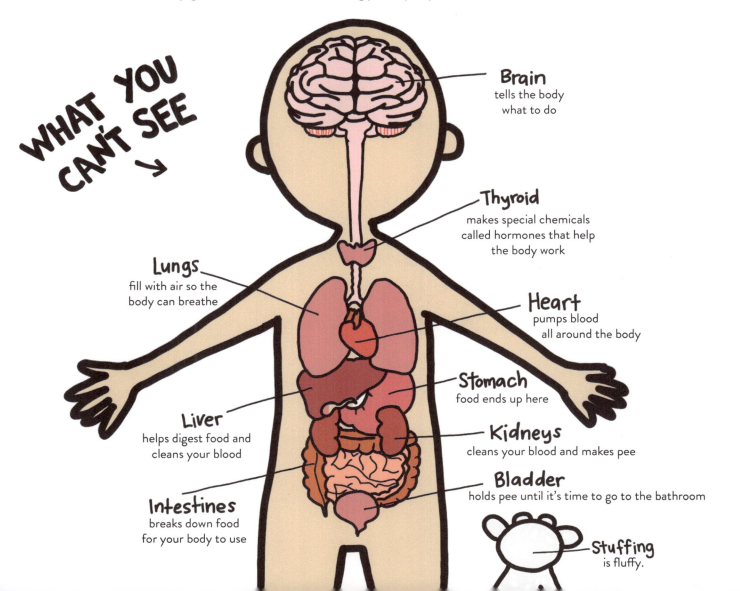

Sometimes these important body parts slow down or stop doing their jobs.
This might happen because the body is old, or it gets hurt,
or the part never really worked quite right since the person was born.

"Welcome to our new club for body parts that aren't working quite right. Please share why you joined!"

"I'd like to make friends who understand what it's like to not work quite right!"

Sometimes we don't *know* why the part stops working.

We *do* know that you can't "catch"
problems with body parts like you can catch a cold.
We also know that there's nothing
a kid could do to make someone's body stop working.

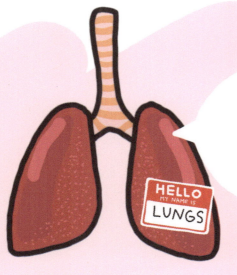

How do people know that their body parts aren't working right?
Usually, people go to the doctor because they notice
something in their body is different than it was before.
Maybe they're having a hard time breathing or swallowing,
or part of their body got bigger or started to hurt, and they don't know why.

Doctors can help people understand *why* they don't feel good.
Doctors are very good at figuring out what's happening inside the body.

They have special tests and can use *really* cool
cameras that take pictures *inside* of the body.

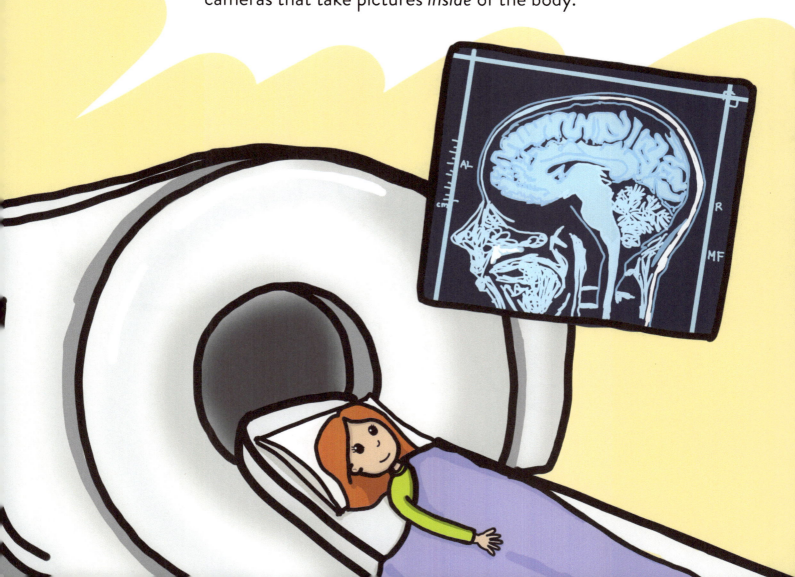

When doctors figure out what's happening inside the body,
they work very hard to help the body work for as long as they can.

They use medicine or machines to make the body parts work better,
or do surgery to remove things that are hurting the body.

Using medicine or surgery helps, but it can't fix everything.
The body part will need to do its job on its own!
Sometimes medicine works for a long time,
and sometimes only for a short time.

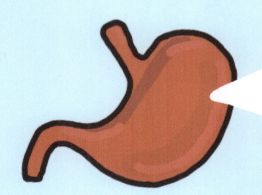

Body parts need to do their jobs and work together for a person to stay alive.
When important body parts can't do their job anymore,
the body will not work, and the person dies.

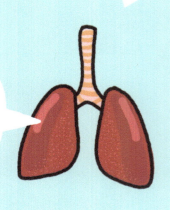

Dying doesn't usually happen right away.
When someone's body is dying,
all of their body parts slowly stop being able to do their jobs.

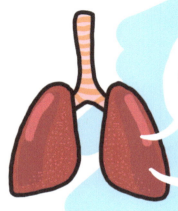

Will the body die today?

Or tomorrow?

We don't know if we have a short time or a long time, it's just not as long as we hoped.

Doctors can usually tell if a body is so sick
that it will stop working and die.
If this is happening to someone you love,
you can trust your grown-up to tell you.

Death happens to all bodies eventually.
But talking or thinking about death,
especially the death of someone you love,
can make you feel a lot of really **BIG** feelings.

When someone you love is dying, there might be a lot of changes.

A special bed might be in their house.
Nurses or other helpers might visit.

They might get medicine to help them feel comfortable.

This is called comfort care or hospice.

Thinking about death
can make us feel scared
or worried
or sad
or angry.

All of these big feelings are normal,
and they happen for both kids and grown-ups.

We call these feelings

GRIEF

Grief is not one emotion. It's a whole bunch of emotions.
Like missing someone, even if they are still here.
Wishing that things were the way they used to be.
Sadness. Loneliness. Anger.

Sometimes we feel these things all at the same time
and it can be **CONFUSING**.

Grief can be confusing, and it can also feel **LONELY** for some kids.
Maybe everyone else feels sad and you feel okay.
Or maybe you feel sad and everyone else is okay.
This can make you feel **ALONE**.

Grief can also feel **GUILTY**.
Some kids feel guilty because they don't
want to be around the person who is dying.
Other kids feel guilty for feeling happy,
like if they really loved the person,
they wouldn't laugh or have any fun.

I think it's time to tell a grown-up about your feelings.

But none of this is true.
We are not alone, even if we sometimes feel that way.
SHARING HOW WE FEEL or what we think makes us feel less alone.

Sometimes kids and grown-ups don't talk about their feelings together.

Maybe grown-ups don't want you to feel sad,
and they don't want you to worry about them.

And maybe you don't share your feelings
because you think it might make your grown-up sad.

And sometimes we don't know what words to use
to share how we're feeling.

You don't always have to *talk* about your feelings.

You can draw. You can ride a bike, or kick a ball outside.

Or you can make a sign, or put out a special rock
when you need people to be extra kind to you.

Grief is not easy to understand or quick to go away like other feelings.
It takes time to get through it.
With grief, there's no right way to feel or act.
And it might change every day.
When this is happening, it's important to take care of ourselves.

Things might not get better right away,
but one day, you **WILL** start to feel better.
Our bodies and brains need different things each day to feel better.
That's why we need to try a bunch of different strategies, like...

Some kids say they feel better
when they can be a helper for the person who is dying.

You can help the person by spending time with them,
watching movies,
reading a book,
playing a quiet game
or giving them a spa day, rubbing their hands with lotion.

Sometimes the person might like to tell you stories about how they grew up,
or share their favorite foods and songs,
or tell you what's important to them.
You can draw pictures and write things down.

Maybe they are the world's biggest basketball fan,
and they keep a giant foam finger on their wall.
Or they work on cars, so their hands are always stained.
Or they keep a special kind of hot sauce in their bag all the time.
Or they smell like a certain kind of flower.

The things that make a person special are part of why you love them.
It's what makes them who they are!

And that never, *ever* goes away.

Hi! My name is Sara. Nice to meet you!

I wrote this book (& lots of others!) because I like to draw + help people.

Things Sara LOVES!
- reading
- Dancing (Badly)
- my family
- nature
- animals
- Quiet time
- Rainbows
- CRUNCHY ICE!

I live in a state known for trees + rain, in a city nicknamed "the cherry city."

I live with my daughter and our three cats, Tater Tot, Waffle, and Batman. One day, I want a **goat**, and a want to name it CAULIFLOWER!

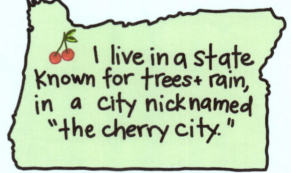

I do all my drawings on an iPad with an Apple pencil

Thank you to Charlie and Audriana for the illustration on page 31.

And my name is Jenni. I help kids when someone they love has a big illness.

I live in the "Grand Canyon" State. Like Sara, I live in my state's capital city.

Things Jenni LOVES! — trees, my family, singing (badly) in the car, military jets, sweets

I work at a famous hospital called Mayo Clinic*.

*The views expressed are the author's personal views, and do not necessarily reflect the policy or position of Mayo Clinic

Hey Parents!

Let's be real:
talking about end of life is HARD.

We get it, and we want to make it easier.

Get this PDF guide for free
at saraolsher.com/cantgetbetter

This guide will help reduce stress
and anxiety for the whole family.

You'll learn how to:
- explain your specific situation;
- answer kids' hard questions;
- connect with your kids;
- encourage open communication;
- build memories and special time together;
- help them cope ongoing.

SCAN THIS USING YOUR PHONE
or visit:at saraolsher.com/cantgetbetter

Copyright © 2024
Sara Olsher
All Rights Reserved.

Book Sara for school visits and public speaking at saraolsher.com

Published by Mighty + Bright
mightyandbright.com

ISBN: 979-8-9867765-5-2

want to tell sara something?
send a letter!

Sara Olsher
13203 SE 172ND Ave
Suite 166, #1121
Happy Valley, Oregon
97086

Milton Keynes UK
Ingram Content Group UK Ltd.
UKHW022120170724
5UKWH00043BA/197

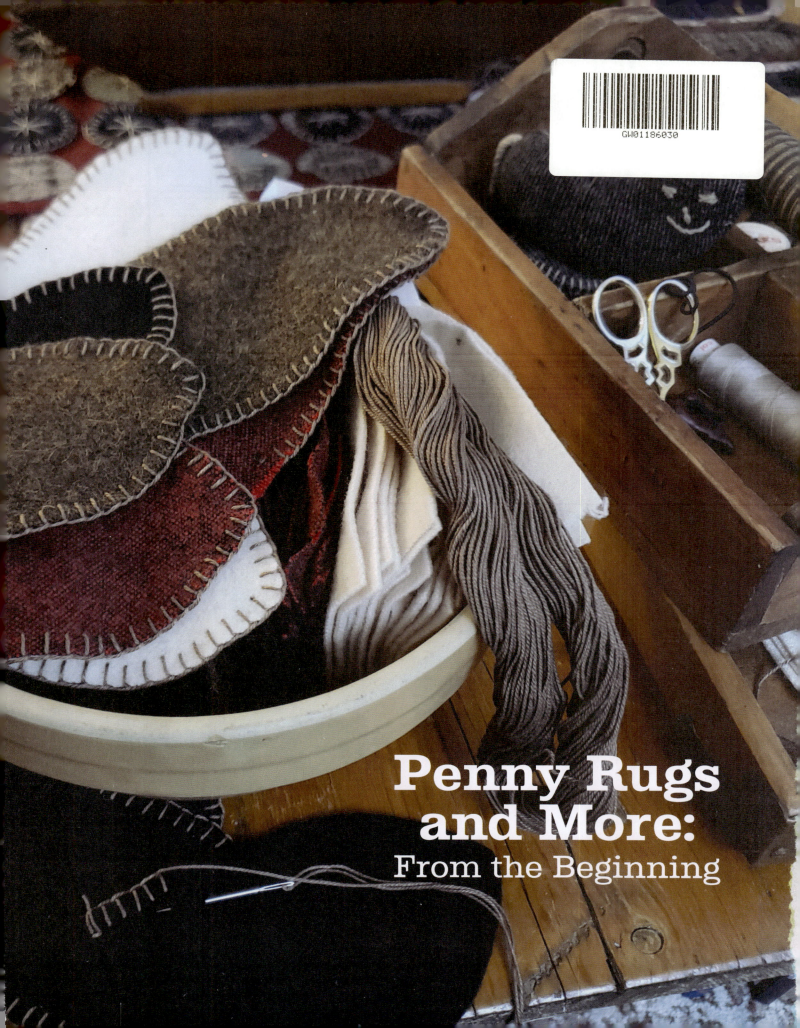

Penny Rugs and More: From the Beginning

Penny Rugs and More:
From the Beginning

COLLEEN MACKINNON

Penny Rugs and More: From the Beginning
Copyright 2023 © Colleen MacKinnon
All rights reserved.

All rights reserved. This book may not be reproduced in whole or in part, stored in a retrieval system, or transmitted in any from or by any means electronic, mechanical or other without written permission from the author, except by a reviewer, who may quote brief passages in a review. For permission to reprint material from the book please contact the author via her social media accounts or email ragamuffincolleen@gmail.com.

Design and graphics: Stride Graphics
Editor: Karen Rempel
Photography: Colleen MacKinnon or as noted.

Printed in Canada and United States
ISBN: 978-1-7782515-0-4

Limit of Liability/Disclaimer of Warranty: Although the author and publisher have made every effort to ensure that the information in this book was correct at press time, the author and publisher do not assume and hereby disclaim any liability to any party for any loss, damage, or disruption caused by errors or omissions, whether such errors or omissions result from negligence, accident, or any other cause.

Use your common sense to avoid injuries or accidents, especially when you are working with bleach, dye, scissors, and needles.

Dedication

To the women in my life that have encouraged me the most.

My mother Eileen and my grandmother Zella

My best friends Marny Young and Missy Caplan

Lindsay MacKinnon, my daughter, an angel without wings

My sister, Taryn Boivin

Cee Rafuse, my dear friend and mentor

And in memory of my husband Neil, my true love and best support.

Contents

A History of Penny & Sewn Rugs	**10**
Examples of Antique Penny Rugs	12
More Resources on the History of Penny Rugs	18
Appliquéd Rugs	18
Wool: The Nature of the Fibre	**20**
Fulling Wool	20
More Tips for Fulling Wool	21
Selvedges	21
Thrifting for Wool	21
Deconstructing Thrift Store Finds	22
How to Handle Interfacing	22
A Word About Moths	22
Washing Wool	23
Washing Thrift Finds and Other Sourced Wool	23
Washing Finished Projects	23
Is It Really Wool?	24
Storing Wool	24
How to Cut Pennies	**26**
Choosing Needle and Thread	**28**
Needles	28
Thread	28
Possible Types of Stitches	29
Dyeing Thread and Fabric	**31**
Preparing Hanks for Dyeing	32
Example 1: Changing the Colour of Yellow and Pale Green Thread	33
Example 2: Marrying Colours Using Onion Skin Dye	34
Example 3: Softening Hues Using Onion Skin Dye	36
Stitching Pennies	**37**
How to Make a "Three-Stack" with a Backing	40
Backing Your Pennies	42
Joining "Backed Stacks" into a Rug	45
Hiding Your Thread: No Knots	46

Beyond the Penny: Using Other Shapes	**47**
Cutting Lamb's Ears or Petals Using Plastic or Paper Templates	47
Blanket Stitching Tongues	48
Binding Tongues	48
Laying Out a Tongue Rug	50
Blind Stitching a Backing or Binding to the Back of a Mat	51
Laying out a Penny Mat	**52**
Working with Plaids	53
Choosing a Background and Sewing the First Pennies	54
Layout Options: One Rug Three Ways	54
Portable Pennies: Organize Your Mat Project to Take and Make	55
Gallery	**56**
There Are No Rules	**64**
Projects and Tutorials	**65**
Mug Rug	65
Candle Mat	66
Bree's Tea Mat	68
Brown Diamonds Mat	72
Finishing with a Binding Edge	75
A Penny for Your Thoughts Mat	78
Beyond the Rug	**82**
Pinch Purse	82
Bookmark	86
Colleen's Make-Do Pincushion	88
Appendix A: Templates	**90**
Circles for Pennies	91
Pinch Purse	93
Make-Do Pincushion	95
Tongue Rug Templates	97
Tongue Rug Layout	99
Bibliography	**111**
References	**112**
Acknowledgements	**114**
Afterword	**118**

Meet the Author

Colleen has been making and creating since she was very little. Her Irish mother taught her to knit and her French-Canadian grandmother taught her to crochet. Along the way were sewing and quilting lessons. Then many years selling her handmade dolls and Santas in craft shows and small shops, and eventually running her own small craft show for several years. All this while raising two beautiful daughters and managing an irrigation service company with her husband for 40 years. During that time came the Internet, opening up new friendships in craft. Colleen found herself buried in stacks of wool and blogging about her exploits. Throughout the past 16 years of making, experimenting, and teaching about penny rugs, Colleen has published many patterns both for herself and for her Nova Scotian friend, penny rug master Cee Rafuse of Early Style Penny Rugs, who has a blog called "The Diary of a Rug Maker."

Never one to be idle, Colleen continues to teach online through her blog, Penny Rugs and More, her Penny Rugs and More Facebook page, and a private Facebook group. Find Colleen selling her patterns and supplies in her Etsy shop 'Penny Rugs and More.'

Colleen lives in historic Fort Langley, British Columbia, Canada.

A History of Penny & Sewn Rugs

Did the original makers of penny mats and rugs collect wool from friends? Cast-offs of family clothing, perhaps mail-order samples from woolen mills or maybe scraps from seamstresses? Collecting until they had enough to create a planned rug, or worked the pieces like a quilt until it was large enough to assemble?

What are critics, collectors, and makers saying?

A penny rug is a compilation of household scraps and the creator's imagination, designed from what was provided or collected. Penny rugs arose from the desire to make something from collected pieces. Not unlike a quilt, a penny rug is a story of the day.

Handcrafted "ruggs," as they were known, were used to cover beds for warmth and to cover table tops or hearths. They were both decorative and useful. Old ruggs have been found in very large sizes showing wear. Is that an indication that they were walked on or just well used on beds, tables, chests, and hearths?

Earlier pieces done on burlap are difficult to find in good condition, as burlap can break down over many years of storage. A large piece of wool was seldom used as a backing because it was too precious.

Not all penny rugs were made of circles. Appliquéd patterns depicting things like animals, people, primitive shapes, flowers, homes, and festive scenes are also known as penny rugs.

Where did handcrafted penny rugs originate? Settlers may have brought rugs and techniques with them from their European homelands.

You can find excellent examples of antique penny rugs in the following publications.

***American Hooked and Sewn Rugs: Folk Art Underfoot* by Joel and Kate Kopp.**
The sewn rugs in their book on pages 123 through 130 are stitched on wool, cotton, or linen. They date from 1835 to early 1900.

The Kopps say, "One form of appliquéd table rug that gained great popularity in the late nineteenth century was the "penny" rug, also called "button" rug, "money" rug, or "coin" rug after the commonplace items the rugmakers used as makeshift templates to trace and cut around. In these rugs, designs were built up either entirely or in large part from the little circles of fabric appliquéd one on top of another to form small target-like pieces that the rugmakers then stitched into endless varieties of geometric patterns."

***Quilts, Coverlets, Rugs & Samplers* by Robert Bishop.**
The two appliquéd rugs in this book are on pages 296 and 297. Both are described as wool on wool.

Bishop says, "Rugs made before 1850 are fairly rare, since many homes had no textile floor coverings well into the 19th century. Made for tabletop or chest, rugs like this were never walked on. Therefore, they are usually in good condition." Then, referring to the second featured rug, Bishop goes on to say, "Few such elaborate early 19th century rugs were made, and of those, even fewer exist today. Not within the means of most collectors, a piece like this is very expensive."

The Craft of Hand-Made Rugs by Ami Mali Hicks

Ami shows the Scalloped Doormat or Tongue Rug on page 53 of her book.

Hicks says, "Its tongue-shaped unit or scallop is cut out of odds and ends of woolen cloth, and sewed on a burlap foundation. These scallops should never be made of cotton as cotton does not wear well with this treatment. The more closely woven the fabric of which the scalloped doormat is made, the more serviceable it is. Loosely woven cloth is apt to fray. Old bits of broadcloth are a satisfactory material to use."

Home Craft Rugs by Lydia Le Baron Walker

Le Baron Walker writes about button, spool, and dollar rugs on pages 235 and 236. In another chapter Lydia goes on to talk about scalloped or petal rugs. Her book is a fascinating look at many hand-made styles of rugs. Lydia includes colour as well as black and white illustrations, and an extensive bibliography.

"The spool, button, or dollar rug is, of structural necessity, a mosaic floor covering, the segments of which are fabric instead of marble, stone, glass, etc. Each bit of material is carefully fitted with the others, and firmly set with stitches. In rugs that have any pretense to beauty, the arrangement of the motifs according to color gives rise to pattern. In the old Colonial rugs, this invariably assumed geometric proportions, diamonds of large or small size being most in favor. While there is a quaint charm about the rugs, the idea that thrift was the inspiration is ever present."

"One is a little at a loss to comprehend why the rugs were not called coin rugs, since those making them took two or three kinds of coin for pattern molds, according to whether there were two or three discs centered one above the other. Perhaps more affluence was expressed by the word "dollar" than by "coin", which might have been interpreted to mean mere "cent". The names "button" and "spool" were acquired through the use of each as a pattern mold, and the three different sizes were usually employed."

In October 1952, on pages 130-134 of **Science and Mechanics** magazine, **Eleanore Engels** writes about using old hats.

She describes making rugs that would be used for floor covers. "For these rugs, use either felt or extra-heavy woolen fabrics (broadcloth or flannel) which don't tend to ravel, or a combination of felt and fabric. You can use lighter weights if you sandwich 2 or 3 layers of cloth together to give proper thickness. You can use all new felt, obtainable by the yard in 72-inch widths, from department stores or mail-order houses; combine it with salvaged materials, such as old hats, discarded billiard and pool table coverings, old

Penny Rugs and More: From the Beginning ☀ 11

college pennants and blankets, industrial felts (from paper mills), and scraps left from the manufacture of athletic goods such as jackets and bowling shirts. (Try Salvation Army store, Goodwill Industries and rummage sales for old hats.) Don't use fur felts or tissue felts—they are too soft to be durable under foot."

When researching, you will find that some rugs have decorative edging, done with elongated pieces resembling the shapes of teardrops and tongues. Tongues may also be known as lamb's ears, tabs, scallops, shoe heels, clam shells, petals, or pen wipers. There is much written about the history of these truly homemade mats and rugs.

Examples of Antique Penny Rugs

These photos are examples of vintage and antique rugs done in penny and tongue styles.

Wonderful embroidered stars highlight this mat.

All pennies sewn onto a feed sack.

Photos on this page are courtesy of April Leas, of Telford, Pennsylvania.

The mat shown to the left has an intricate floral embroidered center. The mat shown below has many rows of multi-coloured tongues, worked with blanket stitches around each tongue and cross stitches to hold the tongues in place. This looks complicated, but it's not. It is, however, a big project. The layout starts with the outermost square row, then layers are added toward the center easing into a circle pattern to finish.

Two tongue rugs. Photos on this page are courtesy of Kara Bowles, Bowles Hilltop Antiques of Markdale, Ontario, Canada.

Penny Rugs and More: From the Beginning 13

A penny mat with tongue finishes, and another with scalloped trimming around the edge. The mat shown above has a diamond center gradiating out to the ends. Notice the attractive geometric star design on the right mat.

Photos on this page are courtesy of Kara Bowles, Bowles Hilltop Antiques of Markdale, Ontario, Canada.

Two more wonderful penny mats with tongue finishes. Playing cards must have been the inspiration for the mat on the right. The mat above has pointed tabs for trim.

Photos on this page are courtesy of Kara Bowles, Bowles Hilltop Antiques of Markdale, Ontario, Canada.

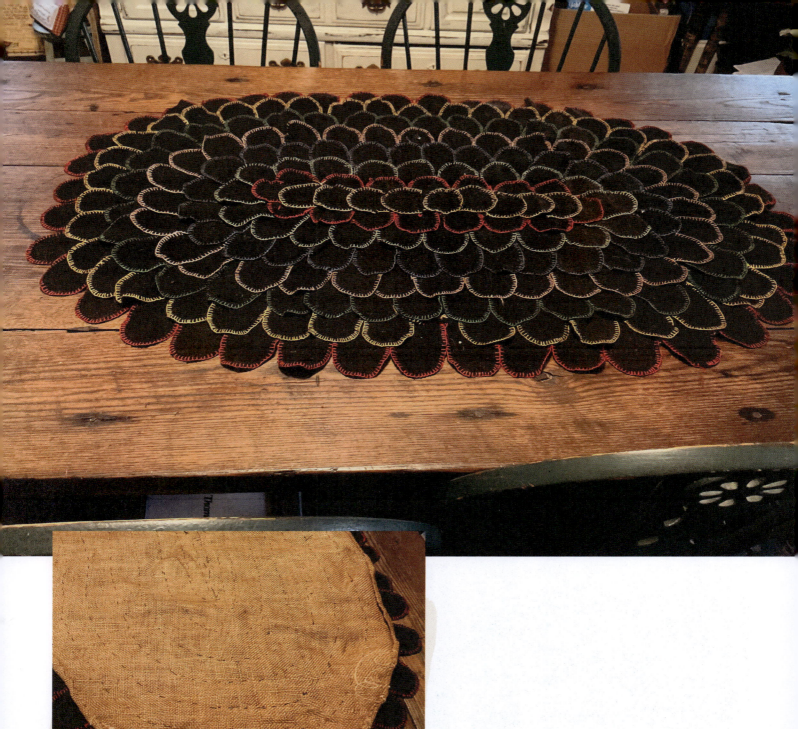

Back of mat above

The mats on these two pages are good examples of burlap used as a base or for the backing. If you are lucky enough to find old mats, the burlap and the stitches are likely to have worn down. Burlap especially does not last.

16 ❁ Penny Rugs and More: From the Beginning

Back of mat above

Delores found these two mats in Canada and added them to her collection. Aren't they gorgeous!

Photos on these two pages are courtesy of M. Delores Tolley Sommers of West Jefferson, North Carolina.

Penny Rugs and More: From the Beginning 17

More Resources on the History of Penny Rugs

You can read more about penny rugs in the Time-Life Books Series, **American Country: The Needle Arts.** See the Bibliography at the end of this book.

Their chapter "For the Table" begins on page 93, with penny rugs and appliquéd rugs shown on pages 96 through 101. "Reaching their peak of popularity around the 1870s, appliquéd table rugs were part of a Victorian fashion for making highly decorative, but largely useless, handicrafts to fill every corner of the home... they were purely ornamental, and might be placed on a parlor table... to create an "artistic" vignette."

The chapter goes on to feature illustrations and various compositions including the penny or "button" rug. The book has a wonderful collection of American needlework illustrations including samplers and bed covers, as well as hooked and braided rugs.

Don't just settle on that issue; look further in the **Folk Arts** edition to find more appliqué rug references. Here again it is mentioned that the rugs were used as coverings for tables and chests instead of being placed on the floor.

Penny rugs are great fun to research. There are many craft magazines and even more recent publications that reference them. Take a look back through your own magazine archives or collections.

Appliquéd Rugs

Appliqué is a technique that is used in making penny rugs. Here is an excerpt about appliqué from the American Folk Art Museum's article, **"The Great American Cover Up: American Rugs on Beds, Tables, and Floors,"** June 5 to September 9, 2007.

"Appliqué is a nineteenth-century term for an earlier needlework technique known as applied-work. Historically, appliqué has had many uses in clothing, upholstery, bed furnishings, and quilts. By the first quarter of the nineteenth century, it had become a popular technique used to make table, hearth, and floor rugs.

"Appliqué involves cutting elements from one fabric and sewing them onto another, larger foundation fabric. The technique lends itself to original geometric or pictorial compositions created through the use of single-layer or multilayered applied elements. Most appliquéd rugs are made primarily from wool, often in dark, saturated colours. Finer details may be added through embroidery and appliqués cut from lighter-weight fabrics.

"By the mid-nineteenth century, appliqué became the basis for a type of table rug known variously as a penny, button, coin, or money rug, whose primary design motif is a circle. The rug could be composed of same-size circles that were cut using a template and repeated across the surface, or of multiple circles cut in graduated sizes. The latter were stacked in decreasing size order, with the smallest on the top, and then sewn onto the foundation. Embroidery, often buttonhole stitching, was usually added around the circumference of each circle. Penny rugs were finished into geometric shapes—square, rectangular, oval, or hexagonal—and remained popular into the twentieth century."

Wool: The Nature of the Fibre

There's nothing like working with wool. It's so forgiving. It's easy to cut, stitch, and dye, letting you focus your attention on your creative ideas.

The question I hear the most when people begin making penny rugs is, "How do I felt wool?"

First, it helps to understand the properties of wool. It is an organic substance. All wool is different, just like the sheep and goats that give up their coats for it.

Looking under a microscope [see figure below], you can see the scales on wool, also called cuticles.

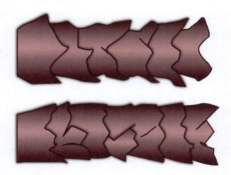

Wool under a microscope

If you treat your wool sweater to a hot wash, the scales will open and then close, never to open again. This process is called fulling, and that's what shrinks the wool when creating felt.

For penny rugs, we don't need to use pure wool. Truly, you can make a penny rug from a fabric that is a blend, or not wool at all. We do love to use something that is soft, durable, and tightly woven. That is the nature of wool when it is fulled or felted. Woven or knit, it is soft and wonderful to work with.

Fulling Wool

Fulling wool is the process of heat and agitation that results in felted wool. Fulled wool frays less and resists further shrinkage.

It has been my experience when fulling wool for penny mats and appliqué to use a warm wash and then a cold rinse. What!? You are saying that everyone told you to use hot water, right or wrong? Here is my cautionary wisdom. Certainly, hot water will full your wool, and oh my, one day you will pull a beautiful cloth from your washer that is so thick you can use it straight away for a doormat. So, before you ruin a gorgeous wool fabric, start with a warm wash and cold rinse.

If your fabric doesn't felt, perhaps it was treated at the factory not to shrink at all. That's a process and a trademark called SuperWash®.

If your wool fabric did felt up, but not as much as you'd like—you might want it thicker and tighter—then go ahead and toss it back in a hot wash. It's been my experience that the agitation and heat

20 ✤ Penny Rugs and More: From the Beginning

will further open the scales and the fabric will be thicker. A hot dryer can further the process, but the fabric will fluff. Perhaps you don't want it fluffy. That's fine; hang it to dry and save the energy expense. Or follow up with a good pressing.

Remember that the process of stitching the wool pieces in place, in circles or other shapes, will hold any loose fibres. So, if the wool is a blend or not completely fulled, your stitches will hold the fibres in place.

That is what wool appliqué and penny rugs are about. Use up and make do. Most of all, enjoy your project!

More Tips for Fulling Wool

- ⊛ Just use a tiny bit of soap or you'll have a washer full of suds.

- ⊛ Never use fabric softener.

- ⊛ Remember to clean the lint trap of your dryer periodically while tumbling.

- ⊛ If your fabric becomes too thick, try a good pressing to flatten it before using in a project.

- ⊛ Most importantly, remember to have fun!

Selvedges

If you have selvedges on yardage pieces, rip or trim them off before fulling. If the fabric is a blend and felts up well, the selvages may become crunched up, the fi-

bres next to them will be bunchy. Use the selvedges to make great rustic ribbons for tying parcels and packages.

Thrifting for Wool

There are lots of reasons to buy recycled wool. It is inexpensive and versatile, and you can find great textures and weaves. You can build a big stash quickly.

I don't recommend sourcing men's jackets... there is far too much interfacing and other fussy construction in them. Look for ladies' skirts, capes, slacks, large lightweight coats, lightweight blankets, and yardage. Yardage likely won't have content tags, so I use the chin test... if it's really scratchy to my chin, it most likely has a high wool content! After working with wool for many years, I am not easily fooled.

Look for 80% or greater wool content as anything less may not completely dye.

- ⊛ Choose wisely; check labels carefully for content.

- ⊛ Avoid SuperWash® wool if you want to felt it.

I recommend that you wash all garments and yardage immediately. This practice will eliminate any moth larvae that might be hidden in the fibres.

Penny Rugs and More: From the Beginning ⊛ 21

Deconstructing Thrift Store Finds

Choose a nice day, or find shelter, and do your garment deconstruction work outside. I don't do this work inside my home as it creates dust and could bring in unwanted pests.

- ✹ With coats, I snip into the lining and waste no time ripping it out, while removing the shoulder pads and any other constructive pieces.

- ✹ Remove the buttons and cut out the zippers; keep these to use on other projects.

- ✹ Skirts are the easiest. I quickly cut out the zipper, then cut off the waistband and remove the lining.

How to Handle Interfacing

Some interfacing just will not come off easily. Sometimes small dots of residue remain. Rather than fuss with it, I leave the interfacing and turn it to the inside or back of my work. If it's too thick to work with, well, I just don't use those pieces.

I've found that if I take the time to open every seam and remove interfacing, I'll have small pieces that bunch up in the wash, ultimately resulting in permanent scrunches or folds that I simply cannot steam iron out. My quick method is to leave the garment in one piece, interfacing intact, unless it is easily torn away. And as a bonus, you can store the garment on a hanger until ready to use!

A Word About Moths

Never bring used wool directly into your home. It must be cleaned before it's stored, as described next.

This applies to your own wool garments as well! Be sure to clean winter sweaters before storing them away for the season.

Sunlight is the bane of textile moths. If you are keeping your wool snug in a closet, do air it out occasionally, shake, refold, and vacuum the space often.

If you have an infestation, do a thorough cleaning. Take all your fabric stash outdoors, air it out, shake it out. Wash anything that has evidence of new damage. Re-store your fabrics, as I note further on, and perhaps invest in some clothes moth pheromone traps.

Fortunately, I haven't had any substantial insect damage, and I hope you won't either. Be careful not to bring unwelcome pests into your home. It's wise to keep your finished projects clean as well and shake the dust out often.

Washing Wool

The procedure for washing used wool in preparation for projects varies slightly from washing your finished projects.

Washing Thrift Finds and Other Sourced Wool

It's important to wash wool before bringing it into your home and using it in projects. Washing your fabric removes potential moth larvae and ensures the colour is fast.

To prepare wool for storage and for use in your projects:

- Toss all pieces into the washer, with a small amount of detergent, for a warm wash, cold rinse.

- Keep like colours together. If you get a "bleeder" you don't want to accidentally over-dye the other fabrics. (A bleeder is a fabric with dye that wasn't fully attached or wasn't set properly.) Shades that could be a problem are reds and bright blues, some greens and blacks. Test any potential bleeder in a cup of boiling water, the water will turn colour as it bleeds the dye.

- Tumble or hang to dry.

Washing Finished Projects

Take care of your finished wool projects just like you care for your favourite sweaters.

To wash your finished projects:

- Hand wash in cold water with a tiny amount of mild detergent.

- Lay flat and squeeze out excess moisture between layers of towels.

- Lay flat to dry.

Is It Really Wool?

There are three tests to confirm if you have wool. Use a small swatch for these tests.

1. Burn

Wool will turn to ash and smell like burned hair. Synthetics will melt and burn quickly. Use caution: Do this outside or over a sink.

2. Bleach

Soak overnight in a small amount of full-strength bleach. Pure wool will disappear by morning; any synthetic component will remain. Do this in a safe place in a covered glass dish or bottle.

3. Rip

100% wool makes a lovely soft tearing sound. If you hear a harsh ripping noise, that means there is another component; the fabric is not 100% wool.

And here's a fourth test... When you full your wool, if it smells like wet dog, well then, it's wool!

Storing Wool

Store wool in cubbies, shelving, or well sealed bins.

Store wool scraps in boxes, bins, baskets, or large reusable sturdy shopping bags. It is a myth that lavender and cedar will ward off moths. Although, you will find sachets of lavender in my studio. I store my fabrics in cubbies and on shelves with good natural light from a window.

You could use zippered fabric storage bags with plastic fronts if you are worried about moths. Or use bins, chests, or blanket boxes being sure they have good tight lids.

Plastic zip bags are useful, but don't leave bagged pennies in direct sunlight... the wool will sweat out the natural lanolin, and soon you'll have a bag full of wet pennies.

How to Cut Pennies

Penny rugs do not need much in the way of supplies. You'll need something round to use as a template, needle, scissors, wool or felt, and some thread.

These projects are very portable, patterns are not necessary. All you need to do is trace circles onto tracing paper.

You can use any circular object for a template:

- Coins
- Spools
- Buttons
- Bottle caps
- Metal washers
- Water glasses

Or create your own templates from medium-weight plastic or chipboard.

> See Appendix A for the Circles for Pennies Template, which has a variety of sizes of circles.

Use freezer paper or brown butcher paper from the grocery store for tracing and cutting fabrics into shapes.

To cut your pennies:

1. Draw circles directly onto the dull side of the freezer paper or waxed butcher paper.

2. Place the freezer or butcher paper SHINY side down on the wool. The shiny side has wax on it.

3. Press for a few good seconds with a hot iron on the steam setting, pressing the entire square of paper. This makes the paper stick to the wool for cutting.

4. Cut the fabric into strips and then into individual square pieces.

5. Carefully cut around the circle, cutting through the paper and the fabric.

6. Remove the paper from the circle.

 Tip: These paper pieces can be ironed again several times.

Another method, is to skip the freezer paper. Just hold the template directly against the fabric, cutting around it. And further to that, a tip from my friend Cee is to use a small piece of double-sided tape to hold your template to the fabric, reuse the tape several times. Experiment with these ideas to find what is good for you.

Penny Rugs and More: From the Beginning 27

Choosing Needle and Thread

The thread you use is an important visual element in your penny rug. You can use any thread that is strong and will fit through the eye of a needle.

Needles

Choose a needle with a large eye and sharp point. I recommend Chenille needle sizes #18, #20, or #22.

Thread

Use dark or light-coloured threads, match or don't match, complement or contrast.

Check your stash for:

- **Embroidery cotton** — use all six plies or split as desired
- **Pearl cotton** — has sheen, is less primitive
- **Crochet cotton** — my preference is #10 (will take dye well)
- **Linen thread** — check the strength
- **Fibres from old clothes or sweaters** — take something apart and see if the fibres make good threads:

  - *threads from monk's cloth (cotton, will not be mercerized); check the strength (will take dye well)*

  - *thread from linen cloth (check the strength)*

- **Butcher's cotton twine** — my friend Cee's favourite; find a lightweight size (will take dye well)
- **Wool threads** — take care not to pull too hard when stitching with wool; also, use shorter lengths of 12-18" (blends will have more strength)
- **Sewing thread** — yes, simple sewing thread, if you prefer not to have a fancy finish. This kind of thread lends itself to whipstitches and it mostly fades into the work, becoming almost invisible when done.

The rug and your stitching style will make the project your own. Let the rug speak to you. Observe, and use the 10-foot rule… drape threads and step away 10 feet. Visualize.

Thread tips:

- Heavier threads will stand out as a design on the rug.
- Lightweight threads show the penny colours.
- Sewing thread is almost invisible.

Remember to save extra thread for repairs, or not. Use up and make do if repairs are needed, like earlier makers.

Possible Types of Stitches

Use a stitch style and thread you are comfortable with. There are no rules.

Some stitching ideas:

- blanket stitch

- variations of blanket stitch, for example, a V blanket stitch will give a lacey look

- whip stitch

- any embroidery stitch that will hold the appliqué in place

To determine the stitching length of thread needed, try three to four times the circumference of a penny.

Penny Rugs and More: From the Beginning 29

Dyeing Thread and Fabric

You may want to dye your thread and fabric to change the colours, or to soften them.

Dyeing fabrics of different colours together helps "marry" the colours, meaning harmonize different colours so they seem to be of similar vibrancy and related tones.

Photo courtesy of Cee Rafuse

Photo courtesy of Cee Rafuse

Preparing Hanks for Dyeing

Before dyeing thread, wind it into a hank.

Tie the hank very loosely in about four places around the hank, using a figure-eight loop that splits the hank. This will hold it together and keep it from tangling while it's in the dye pot. The ties must be loose; if tied too snugly, the dye will not soak in under the ties and you will have undyed bits evenly spaced throughout your thread or yarn.

If you've done other crafts with thread or wool, you may already have a swift—a device for winding thread or wool from its current spindle or ball into a hank.

If you don't have a swift, shown below, use the distance between your hand and bent elbow to wind a hank. Or, turn a chair upside down and use the four legs to wrap around, then tie and remove the finished hank.

Stirring the pot

Drying dyed hanks

Twisted dyed hanks

Example 1: Changing the Colour of Yellow and Pale Green Thread

It's easy to change the colour of light threads and fabrics. I've experimented on blues, whites, beiges, and just about any light colour.

Before dying

Drying dyed hanks

 Some possible dyeing experiments:

- I generally use 350 yards of ecru or other light colours of #10 crochet cotton and one box of Tan Rit dye.

- I have added just a ½ teaspoon of black Tintex™ dye for a darker result that is almost green.

- In yet other trials, i.e., for the orange result, I used KIWI® brand, only 1 teaspoon of their brown dye.

The good news is, these dyes are easily found at grocery or thrift stores. Start a collection, find some light colours of crochet cotton, wind them into hanks or one-yard lengths, then start experimenting. You'll soon have a stash of inexpensive wonderful threads to incorporate into your projects.

Twisted dyed hanks

Penny Rugs and More: From the Beginning ❋ 33

Example 2: Marrying Colours Using Onion Skin Dye

Here is an example of dyeing precut pennies and fabric to soften and marry the colours. Onion skin dye is great for this!

I make onion skin dye following my friend Cee's method:

1. Firmly stuff and fill a slow cooker with collected brown dry onion skins.

    Tip: It may be best to use a slow cooker that you wouldn't use for cooking.

2. Fill with water and cook on low overnight.

* Save the skins to repeat the process for another batch of dye; it will be lighter.

* Keep any leftover dye in a jar in the fridge until ready to use again.

* You can test your dye strength by taking a half cup of dye from the crockpot and a half cup of boiling water. Into this diluted dye place a piece of string or wool to soak overnight and then rinse. This gives you an idea of how much plain water to add to the full-strength dye.

* Onions skins can vary season to season, harvest to harvest. The longer they are stored the darker the skins, and ultimately the dye.

My finished batch of dye

3. In my large dye pot, I mixed equal parts onion skin dye and water.

4. I added about ¾ of this box of mixed pennies—hundreds of them! Notice the rogue green....it was a good "bleeder." I left the green in the pot purposely; I hoped to mix in dye that might bleed from that green.

7. It didn't take long for the water to become almost clear; the dye was absorbed. Again, this will vary, don't worry if all the dye is not soaked up.

8. At this point I rinsed and rinsed, squishing out the water.

   Let them drip dry in a strainer over your sink, or lay out on a towel overnight.

9. I straightened and stacked them while they were damp. Ironing and trimming as needed.

5. After bringing the pot to a full steam, heating, and stirring for about 15 minutes, I added about 1/2 cup of white vinegar and a couple tablespoons of salt. Both will help to drive the dye into the fabric. It's a myth that they will set the dye.

6. I stirred well, turned off the heat, and let it rest for a couple of hours.

Note: Dyeing wool pennies after they've been cut gives them a more worn, primitive look. See how the green pennies left their dye randomly throughout, creating a worn colouring.

Penny Rugs and More: From the Beginning 35

Example 3: Softening Hues Using Onion Skin Dye

For the next experiment, I went back to the dye pot and made another batch of onion skin dye.

1. I mixed 1 part onion skin dye to 10 parts water.

2. When the bath was ready I added this batch of mixed pink pennies with some uncut pieces of yellow, green, and blue wool.

3. After adding vinegar and salt, stirring well and letting the batch rest for a few hours, the dye was well absorbed and the water was clear.

4. I rinsed and squished the water out in the sink.

Result: The onion skin dye softens and marries the colours and unifies them for use in one project.

36 ❋ Penny Rugs and More: From the Beginning

I invite you to experiment with dyes of your choices. Read and research. You may really enjoy the process of dyeing wool. My methods may not be your methods.

Dyeing Tips
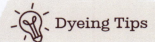

- Check dyes for toxicity; perhaps you won't want to use them indoors and you'll want to wear a mask.

- With any dye, natural or chemical, always be cautious and read directions carefully.

- Never use the same utensils and pots that you would use for cooking.

- Be sure to use a pot that is not copper, iron, or aluminum.

Stitching Pennies

Let's begin with some examples of stitching pennies onto your backing fabric. Take a look through these pictures for a visual overview of different techniques, and then we'll get into specifics.

The first stitch:

Penny Rugs and More: From the Beginning

Closed blanket stitch:

Reverse blanket stitch:

Making a decorative star:

Stitching single pennies:

38 ❂ Penny Rugs and More: From the Beginning

Stitching down a stack:

Penny Rugs and More: From the Beginning ❁ 39

How to Make a "Three-Stack" with a Backing

Stacking pennies gives you more design options and new ways to mix colours. You can stack two or three pennies, or more.

Here I'll show you how to make a stack of three with a backing. I stacked 1", 1 ½", and 2 ¼" pennies in this example.

To make a three-stack:

1. Measure enough thread to completely stitch around both the first and the second penny without stopping.

A rule of thumb is 3-4 times the circumference should be enough thread. You'll know, after you fall into a rhythm with your stitching, just how much thread is perfect for you.

2. Begin with a 1 ½" penny. Anchor your thread with a back-stitch.

3. Bring the thread through the penny and begin your blanket stitch to attach the 1" to the 1 ½" penny.

4. Blanket stitch around the smaller penny to join the two together.

5. Estimate your last few stitches and equal out the spacing as you near the end of the round.

6. When you reach the beginning, put the needle through the top of the first stitch and bring the needle out the back.

7. Hold the finished stack on top of a 2 ¼" penny and begin stitching around the brown 1 ½" inch penny.

8. Stitch around the stack, attaching it to the 2 ¼" penny.

Here is the needle at the end of the round, going over the first stitch and through to the back of the largest penny.

9. Back stitch to end off your thread.

Penny Rugs and More: From the Beginning ❈ 41

Backing Your Pennies

Now that you've finished the three-stack, you can add a backing to hide the stitches on the back of the largest penny. Use another 2 ¼" penny in the same colour.

To add a backing:

1. Use a back stitch to begin another thread.

2. Blanket stitch the new 2 ¼" penny to the back of the stack.

42 ✹ Penny Rugs and More: From the Beginning

3. When complete, pass your thread from the last stitch through the first top loop of the first stitch.

4. Pass the needle between the layers and pull it out at the back, in the middle of the penny.

5. Push the needle back through the same exact hole, in a different direction, and into some wool in the inside of the stack...you want to grab into some of the inside wool.

6. Do this several times, making a hidden back stitch each time inside the stack.

7. Pull and snip the thread.

Completed three-stack with a backing.

Joining "Backed Stacks" into a Rug

This is an easy way to make a backless rug, as the pennies are already backed.

To join backed stacks:

1. Arrange your pennies into the layout you want to use. See Layout Options: "One Rug, Three Ways" for ideas, on page 54.

2. Use several whip stitches in one place to join the pennies together. Travel through the inside of the stack to the next position, create another set of whip stitches, and so on.

 Tip: A word about the thickness of stacks. Vary wool thicknesses throughout your stacks and throughout the mat. For example, use a thick penny in a 3 stack but don't use 3 thick pennies in one stack and then put a 3 stack of thin pennies next to it. Penny mats and rugs are all about using up and making do, experiment with your fabrics to get the look that you'd like.

Penny Rugs and More: From the Beginning 45

Hiding Your Thread: No Knots

You can use this technique in any situation where you don't want your stitches to show. Here I show you an example of hiding knots on a mat that has wool pennies stitched to a cotton backing.

After bringing the needle out the back of your work:

- ❋ Take a few stitches into the back of the stack, being particular that the tip of the needle goes into the same space as it came out, but in a different direction.

- ❋ When you do this, pick up a bit of the wool stack inside.

- ❋ Then snip the thread close. It pops inside. No knots... a hidden backstitch!

Beyond the Penny: Using Other Shapes

As I mentioned in "A History of Penny and Sewn Rugs," not all penny rugs were made of circles. This section shows you how to work with tongues and petal shapes. These shapes are also known as lamb's ears, tabs, shoe heels, scallops, clam shells, or pen wipers.

Cutting Lamb's Ears or Petals Using Plastic or Paper Templates

See Appendix A for a Tongue Rug Tabs Template.

To make rounded tongues or petal shapes:

1. Cut rectangles to the finished length you want.

2. Hold a plastic or paper template to the end and trim the curve.

 Pro tip: Fold a paper template, hold against your folded wool (matching the folds), and trim.

See "How to Cut Pennies" for other tips.

Penny Rugs and More: From the Beginning 47

Blanket Stitching Tongues

Blanket stitching gives an attractive visual element to your design, while also preventing the edges from fraying over time.

Binding Tongues

Here is a favourite and really quick method for finishing a shape with bias trim. This is one of the cleverest tricks I've learned from my dear friend Cee.

This method lets you skip the entire process of folding and ironing the piece.

To attach bias trim to a tongue:

1. Sew the bias-cut strip of fabric to the front of the felt shape.

2. After sewing the binding strip in place, soak the tongue in water.

3. Fold the trim over to the back of the shape, and fold again to tuck the edges under. Because it's wet, you can shape and place it easily.

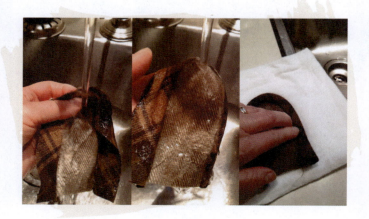

Try it, you will be amazed.

The upside: Quick results with no burned fingertips from turning and ironing.

The downside: Lots of wet pieces of wool drying on towels all over the house overnight.

4. Once dry, finish with a blind stitch and press if needed.

For more information: Check the internet for great tutorials on how to make continuous bias binding. It's truly a clever and quick way to make yards and yards.

Making a Continuous Bias Strip

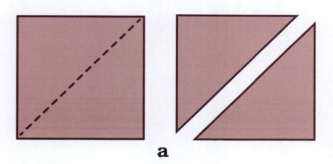

a

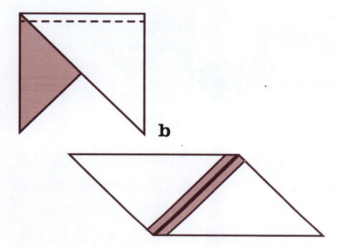

b

Bias edges

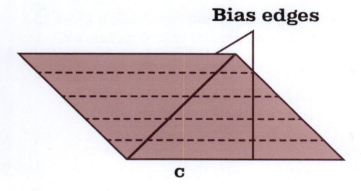

c

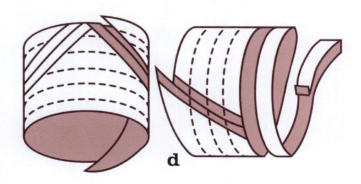

d

Penny Rugs and More: From the Beginning ❁ 49

Laying Out a Tongue Rug

See Appendix A for the Tongue Rug Templates and Layout.

Start with the outer row of the mat. Use more or fewer tongues to create the size you desire. Overlap slightly at the curves. Pin the tongues in place.

Row 1:

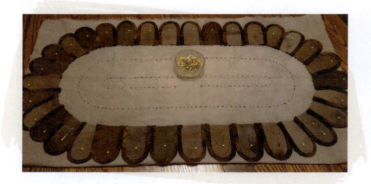

Row 2:

Stagger each row in a brick pattern.

Row 3:

As you work, unpin and adjust if needed. Step back often and review placements.

When you're happy with the placement of all the rows, stitch it all down, one row at a time.

To finish the center, place wider tongues and blind stitch a long double ended tongue along the center of the rug. This will finish the front of the rug.

Then trim and bind the backing, as shown in the next section.

Enjoy your beautiful new rug.

Blind Stitching a Backing or Binding to the Back of a Mat

Blind stitching is the best technique for sewing a backing or binding to your mat. Use a fine needle and thread. The stitch is almost invisible, hidden under the folded edges. Make sure you just catch a few threads of the fabric each time the needle goes through the fold, and take care not to push the needle to the front layer of the piece.

Laying out a Penny Mat

This section gives you many layout ideas.

This mat uses 3", 2", and 1" pennies sewn into three-stacks. The stacks form a rectangular design. See a full tutorial on my blog.

This mat uses 3" and ¾" pennies to form flowers. See page 19 for the finished mat.

Thread guide: When cutting the thread length to sew around a penny onto the mat, use 3-4 times the circumference of the penny.

The mat above uses 2" and 1 ½" pennies sewn into two-stacks. The stacks are laid down in nested lines, with a hexagon shape.

The finished mat is shown on the front and back cover, and in the gallery on page 60.

52 ❁ Penny Rugs and More: From the Beginning

Working with Plaids

The possibilities with plaid are almost endless. Colours are already selected for you to make a coordinated mat. Cut circles from the different colours and start arranging.

Choosing a Background and Sewing the First Pennies

Sometimes it's hard to decide which colour will look best for your background. If in doubt, lay it out!

Choose background colour

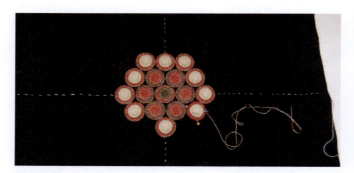

Start at the center

To start sewing pennies to the backing:

1. Mark the center of the rug with basted running stitches.

2. Stitch stacks onto the backing from the center outward, using the basted running stitches as guides.

Layout Options: One Rug Three Ways

This example uses many backed stacks in shades of creamy off whites. Try arranging your pennies in different ways. Here are three possibilities.

Pick the pattern you prefer, then whip stitch them together. See "Joining Backed Stacks into a Rug" on page 45.

Portable Pennies: Organize Your Mat Project to Take and Make

planning is done, it's all about enjoying the stitching.

To take and make wherever you go, thread tiny pennies together. Then you can pull off one group, or one piece at a time to stitch. This is the fun part that makes penny rugs so portable, having no pattern to constantly refer to. Once the

Gallery

Look through this gallery of mats that I've made. I hope you can find ideas and inspiration. Many of the mats included here are featured on my blog and YouTube channel. I have patterns for many of the rugs in my Etsy shop.

Shades of green

This green rug tutorial is on my blog: https://pennyrugsandmore.blogspot.com/

'Poinsettia Mat' The pattern for this mat is in my Etsy shop: https://www.etsy.com/shop/pennyrugsandmore

This is the "A Penny for Your Thoughts" mat. See the "Projects and Tutorials" section of this book for step-by-step instructions.

Find the 3D star tutorial on my blog and April's Petal Mat pattern in my Etsy Shop.

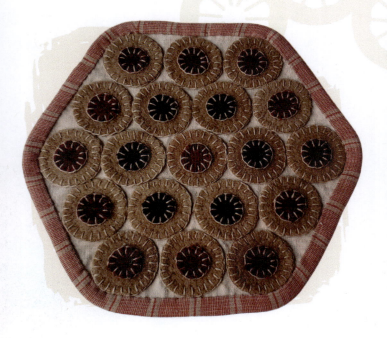

Small mat with bound edge. Wool pennies on cotton foundation with cotton binding.

Create an oval of wool and overlap stacks around the edge.

This mat is easy to make in any size. You don't need a pattern. It's made entirely using backed stacks.

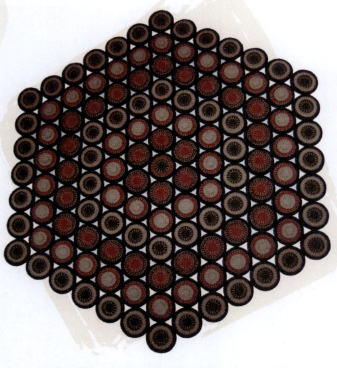

These are all backed stacks whip stitched together.

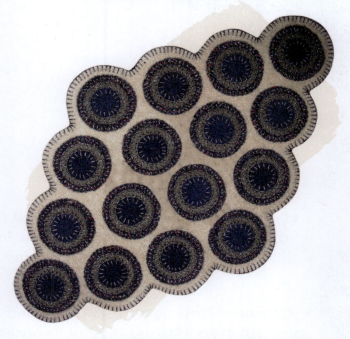

Stitch single, two-stack, or three-stacks to a backing. Carefully trim around the edge and finish with more stitching. This creates a scalloped edge. All the stitching on this mat shows on the back.

Square tongue mat with round center. Look for "April's Petal Mat," available in my Etsy shop.

Penny Rugs and More: From the Beginning 59

The "Plaid Pennies and Tongues" mat, pattern also available in my Etsy shop.

*Backed stacks, whip stitched together.
Find my e-pattern in my Etsy Shop.*

The "Large Hit or Miss" round mat; the pattern is in my Etsy shop.

"Kitty's in the Garden,"
pattern available in my Etsy shop.

"Sunflower in Moonlight,"
pattern available in my Etsy shop.

Penny Rugs and More: From the Beginning

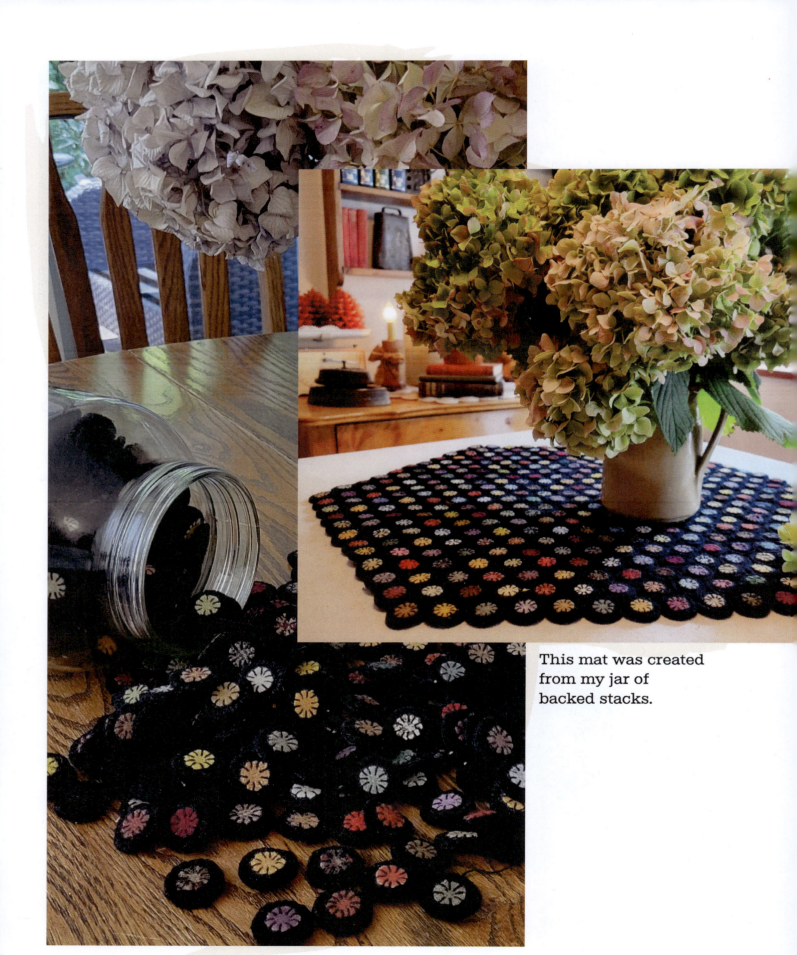

This mat was created from my jar of backed stacks.

62 Penny Rugs and More: From the Beginning

I have to include this gorgeous doily-like mat, it has so many small intricate pieces.

It is so well planned and painstakingly pieced. What a treasure it would be to own this!

Photos are courtesy of April Leas with permission from the antique dealer she met on her travels.

Penny Rugs and More: From the Beginning 63

There Are No Rules

There are no rules for the size of your pennies, colour or style, shapes, fabric choice, or thread.

- ✺ Use what you have, have what you use. If you can pass a needle through it, use it!
- ✺ Use either the right side or wrong side of wool.
- ✺ You don't have to use wool at all; use what the mat calls for in appearance and colour.
- ✺ Combine colours and shapes.
- ✺ Your stitching style is your signature.
- ✺ The rug will tell you what it needs.
- ✺ Your rug doesn't have to have bound tongues; they could be stitched.
- ✺ The pennies don't have to be in straight rows, alternate them.
- ✺ You'll find your rhythm so don't fret about the quality of your work, spacing, or evenness of your stitches.
- ✺ Relax with your stitching, let the project lead you.
- ✺ Mats do not need to have a wool base.

  Many of the old ones were stitched to feed sacks or burlap. (Though burlap is generally very coarse, difficult to stitch through, and does not stand up well to time.)

  Experiment with cotton and blends.

  Try wool flannel as well, it makes a lovely base and is lightweight enough to be used for binding.

- ✺ The edges of your mat can be finished with crochet, or braiding; binding is not necessary. Finish it your way.

 The lesson is... you can make any rug. See it, be inspired, imagine it, and make your own version. Challenge yourself.

Projects and Tutorials

This section shows you eight different fun projects that you can use or adapt. I've sprinkled lots of tips in the projects, so you can learn something even if you don't want to follow the particular pattern. The final three projects take you away from penny rugs, into other possibilities for the techniques you've learned.

Mug Rug

Mug rugs are so easy and a great way to use up scraps.

Materials

- 38 x 1" black pennies
- 19 x 9/16" pennies
- Black #10 crochet cotton

How To

1. Make 19 two-stacks.
2. Back the stacks with 1" black pennies.
3. Whip stitch the 19 backed stacks together.

Penny Rugs and More: From the Beginning   65

Candle Mat

This is a quick little project that doesn't take much wool.

Materials

- Use 19 x 1 ½" wool circles and 19 x ¾" inch circles.
- My thread of choice is black #10 crochet cotton.
- My base square started out at 9 ½" x 9 ½". You can use any fabric for the base, just be sure it is thin enough to work with.

How To

1. Fold and press your base fabric to create a center point, or baste a horizontal and a vertical line in a dark thread.

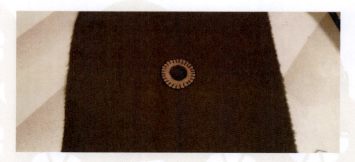

2. Stitch a penny stack in the middle, then work outwards from there.

3. Nest the penny stacks together and adjust your stitch direction as you work around each stack.

4. Keep adding pennies until the layout is complete.

5. Measure off the edges around the pennies with masking tape to trim away excess backing fabric.

This tip comes from my friend Cee at Early Style Penny Rugs.

6. Trim with scissors around the outside edge of the masking tape.

7. Remove the tape.

8. Fold, iron, and pin the edges.

9. Blind stitch with matching sewing thread.

10. My base is wool, so I pressed and steamed the finished mat with a pressing cloth. (Pressing with a cloth directly onto the wool prevents a permanent sheen.)

Penny Rugs and More: From the Beginning ❋ 67

Bree's Tea Mat

Bree's Tea Mat

Here's a lesson for a quick mat. Once you have your colours planned and circles cut, this will stitch up quickly. With large pennies, this mat finishes at a nice size of 15 ½" x 18".

Materials

- Sizes and colours of pennies:
  - 18 x 2 ½" red
  - 19 x 2 ½" gold
  - 6 x 2" brown
  - 1 x 2" red
  - 24 x 1" brown
  - 6 x 1" red
- Approximately 65 yards of #10 crochet cotton
- Very lightweight fabric for the backing

At first, I thought the fabric was too lightweight, but then I really enjoyed working on it and will likely use this weight again.

Make Your Penny Two-Stacks

- 18 x 1" brown on 2 ½"" red
- the rest on 2 ½" gold

Review this photo for the colour and layout of the two-stacks.

How To

68 Penny Rugs and More: From the Beginning

1. Find the center of your fabric, and begin with the center stack—the single 2″ red on gold.

2. Stitch on the remaining pennies, following the pattern shown previously on page 68.

3. When all stitches are completed, press your mat on the reverse side.

4. Lay masking tape carefully around the mat.

 Pro tip: Tape is a quick easy way to achieve an even edge. The tape here is 3/4″ wide, which makes the perfect hem when folding the thin base fabric I used.

You may like to use 1″ tape on a thicker fabric. Try 1″ first; you can always trim it back further if need be.

5. Trim away excess fabric.

6. Remove the tape.

7. Fold and **press** a hem to the reverse side.

Here is a close up of blind stitching the folded hem on the reverse of mat.

The pressed hem is held in place with a 3/4″ appliqué pin.

8. Blind stitch the hem in place.

Final note: I did not line this mat to cover the backside and hide my stitches; I simply turned a 3/4″ hem.

Penny Rugs and More: From the Beginning 69

You can see your stitches on the back. And stitches highlighted on the front as well.

70 Penny Rugs and More: From the Beginning

Brown Diamonds Mat

With this tutorial, I want to share with you the decisions I made as I worked on a mat and made adjustments along the way. In the end, I loved the result! I also show you in detail how to sew a binding edge on a mat.

The finished size of this "Brown Diamonds" mat is approximately 25" x 14". I used pennies that are 1 ½" and ¾" to make two-stacks of red and brown, on tan.

I started stitching this one on the diagonal… and then I struggled. I realized I much prefer to stitch in straight nested lines. I pulled off all my diagonal tape and reset my tape from left to right.

I like to lay out the pattern, tape my rows and number them.

 Remove some of the adhesive of the tape by pressing it against another fabric or cloth, then when pulling the pennies away they will not shred at the edges.

If tape isn't your thing, you can baste the rows without attaching them, or you can string your stacks together and set aside. I just like to avoid pinning it all down.

After taping my pennies into workable rows, I lift away each row and safely set them in a bowl or basket.

Then I start stitching one stack at a time, one row at a time.

After I changed my approach, I really enjoyed stitching this mat. It was fun to do a reverse blanket stitch.

As I stitch, I tend to use just one or two small appliqué pins as I travel along the mat. My favourite size is ¾". This short size keeps my thread from catching, mitigates pokes, and allows me to adjust the stacks as I go.

I am always adjusting and checking alignment.

 Tip: You can also make light pencil or graphite lines. For beginners this can be very helpful.

Wool is so nice to work with, it's so forgiving, you can snug and adjust it easily, even if a penny is not lined up exactly right.

Penny Rugs and More: From the Beginning

My preferred method is to attach the small penny to the larger one and then attach the stack to the rug. This method allows me to travel with my work and then bring the finished stacks together again for assembly. If you prefer to do it the other way around, that's fine. You could stitch all the large pennies down and then go back and stitch the top ones. It's up to you.

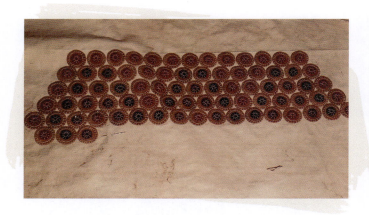

Notice that I folded and pressed my base fabric to create a line to follow.

Look closely at the top edge of the top row. On other tutorials on my blog, you may see that I've stitched a basting line as a guide. You can do either, or both.

At this point, I decided that I really wanted the brown diamonds to have points. These interrupt the red border.

I removed the red pennies and replaced them with brown.

Working row by row, I adjust and nest each penny. The trick is to get that first row nice and straight.

All stacks are complete. Now it's time to cut away the excess base fabric. It's so quick to mask off the edges with 1" wide masking tape. It's a perfect width to plan a border; there's not too much excess to trim away later, and it's the right width to simply turn and hem.

74 • Penny Rugs and More: From the Beginning

Tip: Gently remove the tape after you cut away the fabric beyond it.

Finishing with a Binding Edge

To trim this mat, I wanted to use a dark brown edge for a strong contrast. To make the binding, I cut strips of a lightweight brown wool blend into two long 1 ½" strips and joined them with a bias.

How To

After you have created the bias binding tape, see page 49, fold it in half lengthwise and press, then fold each long side to meet in the center, and again, press.

I pinned the bias binding tape around the mat, close to the last row of penny stacks, minding that the bias joins would be on the long sides.

I back stitched this in place by hand all the way around the mat.

Penny Rugs and More: From the Beginning 75

I folded one end on a bias until the end touched the side, creating a triangle as shown on the left strip.

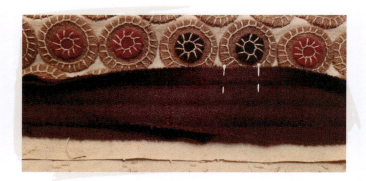

Then I lay the opposing end over the folded end, and pinned it in place.

Next, I pinned and sewed on the bias to join the ends of the binding.

I trimmed away the excess.

 Tip: You can also use a small running stitch or your machine.

I left a few inches open, not stitched to the mat, and a few inches excess binding at each end.

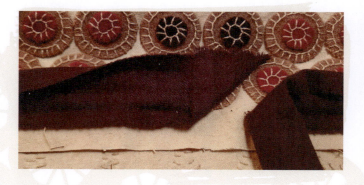

Penny Rugs and More: From the Beginning

I pressed the edges of the seam open, pinned the section of binding to the mat, and finished attaching the strip.

At this point I needed to trim away excess backing fabric, using the binding as a guide for cutting.

I folded the binding over and pinned it to the mat, easing at the corners, using the stitching lines as my guide.

Finally, I made tiny blind stitches to hold the binding to the back of the mat, following the stitching line.

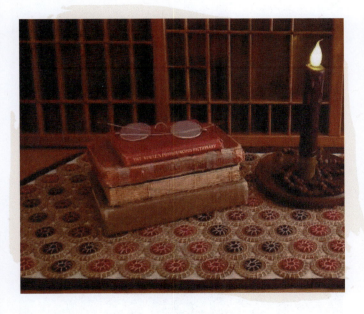

Penny Rugs and More: From the Beginning

A Penny for Your Thoughts Mat

This tutorial takes you through the process I used to lay out, design, and assemble this mat.

I wanted to use a random layout of 1" greens and reds for my "Penny for Your Thoughts" mat. I arranged and rearranged the pennies until the colours felt right.

It's not easy to be random! I taped the rows and numbered them so I wouldn't forget my random layout.

I hand-basted the center row down to hold it in place.

78 ✺ Penny Rugs and More: From the Beginning

I used a French knot to hold the pennies in place and worked a closed blanket stitch around them.

I gathered the rows into a container for storage between crafting sessions. Wood or cardboard cigar boxes are great!

A simple closed blanket stitch. Do you see the V?

How To: Working on an angle, join the bottom of each blanket stitch. End the circle with the needle into the first stitch.

Penny Rugs and More: From the Beginning ✺ 79

After sewing on all the pennies, I applied masking tape to all sides to create an even cutting edge. I trimmed away the excess fabric, using the tape as a guide, then gently removed the tape.

I wanted to use a backing for this mat, so I laid the mat right-side-down onto the backing fabric.

I trimmed away the excess backing fabric, matching the two pieces in size.

Next I pressed the backed mat with a warm iron.

I placed the right sides together and pinned all sides. I could have stitched the pieces together by hand. I chose to use my machine, leaving a 2-3″ opening on one side for turning.

I trimmed the seams down to ½″ and clipped the corners. Depending on the type of fabric and its tendency to fray, ¼″ might be enough of a seam.

 Pro Tip: After you turn your mat inside out, be careful with the corners. Use something blunt to push them out. Or you can pull them gently from the outside with a strong needle.

Finally, I sewed the opening closed with an invisible ladder stitch. You can also use a tiny whip stitch.

Penny Rugs and More: From the Beginning   81

Beyond the Rug

Pinch Purse

See Appendix A for the Pinch Purse Templates.

This pinch purse is also known as a clam shell, a pipkin, a thimble holder, or a Victorian sewing box. Some call it a Brazil nut, others call it a beechnut, and still others make them for Christmas ornaments. Not only for holding thimbles, they are a nice size to tuck a tiny gift into and hang on a tree.

Materials

- Lightweight plastic or cardboard for liners
- Pen or pencil
- Fabric for outside
- Fabric for lining
- Needle and thread
- Optional: batting

How To

From the large petal template:

- Cut 3 of outer fabric and 3 of lining fabric

From the small petal template:

- Cut 3 of batting
- Cut 6 lightweight plastic or cardboard for a firm liner (trim 3 petals by a scant 1/8")

2. Cut 3 pieces of batting from the smaller template.

   Note: Batting is only necessary if you want a puffy soft outer side.

3. Layer the batting between the fabric and the plastic or cardboard liner piece.

1. Make a running stitch around the edges of the larger shape.

   ✸ In the above photo I've traced the smaller shape onto the larger, so you can see where to make the running stitch, between the edges of the smaller and larger shapes. And skip a stitch across the points.

4. Use a needle to pull up the running thread and gather the fabric around the petal.

5. Fold and flatten the fabric at the corners and tack both ends in place.

    Pro Tip: Run some stitches from one side to the other side. This also helps tighten the fit.

6. Repeat steps 3-5 to make 2 more fabric-covered petals with batting for the larger outer pieces and 3 with no batting for the smaller inner pieces.

Penny Rugs and More: From the Beginning ✸ 83

❋ Here is the reason the inner lining petals should be smaller than the outer pieces. It helps with assembly to have the liner edges displaced from the edges of the outer petal.

8. Position the liners on the other 2 petals as shown here:

Left, center, and right petals.

❋ Notice how the lining of the center petal is centerd. The other two, left and right, are displaced slightly off center.

7. Use tiny whip stitches all around the petal to join a slightly smaller inner liner to an outer petal.

❋ Remember, you've trimmed 3 of your plastic petals by a scant 1/8" to use for the inside of the purse (liners).

84 ❋ Penny Rugs and More: From the Beginning

9. Using a decorative thread, whip-stitch the wider displaced edge of the left petal to the center petal using a simple whip stitch.

10. Now whip-stitch the wider displaced edge of the right petal to the other side of the center petal.

11. On the third side, the opening, whipstitch up from each point just a bit.

12. Make a strong overcast tack stitch. You're done!

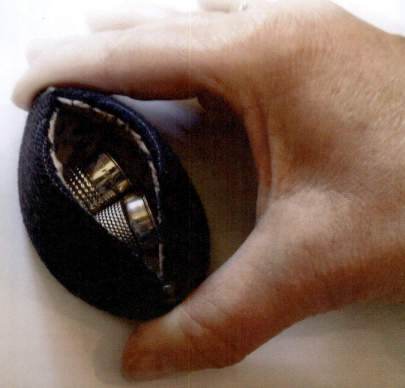

Bookmark

These are simple and very useful. You will love this style of bookmark, I do!

Materials

- 16" of elastic cord
- A variety of beads and/or buttons
- Two 1" wool pennies
- One ½" or 9/16" wool penny
- Needle and thread

How To

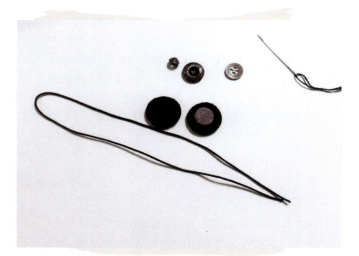

86 ❊ Penny Rugs and More: From the Beginning

1. Thread the beads and buttons onto the doubled cord, then knot the end and trim.

2. Secure the knot onto one of the 1" wool pennies.

3. Then stitch the smaller penny onto the 1" penny to hide any stitches.

4. Stitch the second 1" penny to the back of the stack, enclosing the knot.

5. Make some back stitches inside the stack to secure your thread, and snip.

The beads or buttons can be adjusted to shorten the cord for smaller books.

Penny Rugs and More: From the Beginning ❁ 87

Colleen's Make-Do Pincushion

Materials

- Wool fabric
- Large button
- Strong thread
- Stuffing of your choice; fibre fill or raw wool
- 5-6" inch thrifted glass candle holder
- Glass etching compound – you can find this in many craft locations
- Dark stain to age the glass
- Clear matte finish spray
- Tea bags or instant tea (without sugar)
- 4" wide by 16-18" length of cheese-cloth

How To

1. Use the template in Appendix A to cut 5 pieces of matching wool.
2. Pin the pieces together so that all 5 pieces join at the pointed end, creating a ball, with the wide end as the opening at the bottom.
3. Sew the right sides together with a ¼" seam allowance.
4. Turn right-side out and attach a large button to the center top. Stuff.
5. Etch a candle holder with glass etching compound.

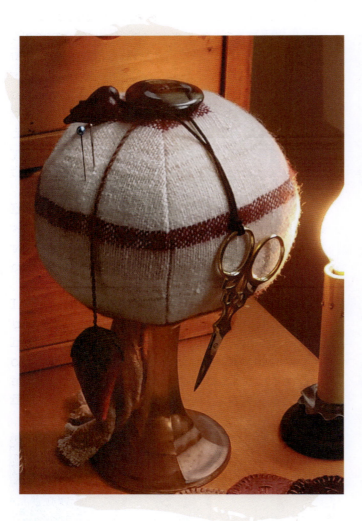

See Appendix A for the Make-Do Pincushion Template.

6. Rub the candle holder with dark stain to age it further.

7. Let it dry and seal with a clear, matte finish spray.

8. Use a strong thread to gather the base of the pincushion, insert the candle holder, and tie off snugly.

9. Tea dye the cheesecloth. (Make a strong tea bath, soak well to age, and then rinse and dry.)

10. Tie the cheesecloth at the base of the pincushion and glue or stitch it to hold it in place.

11. Optional: Hang your favourite stitching scissors and/or an emery strawberry from the button.

Circles for Pennies

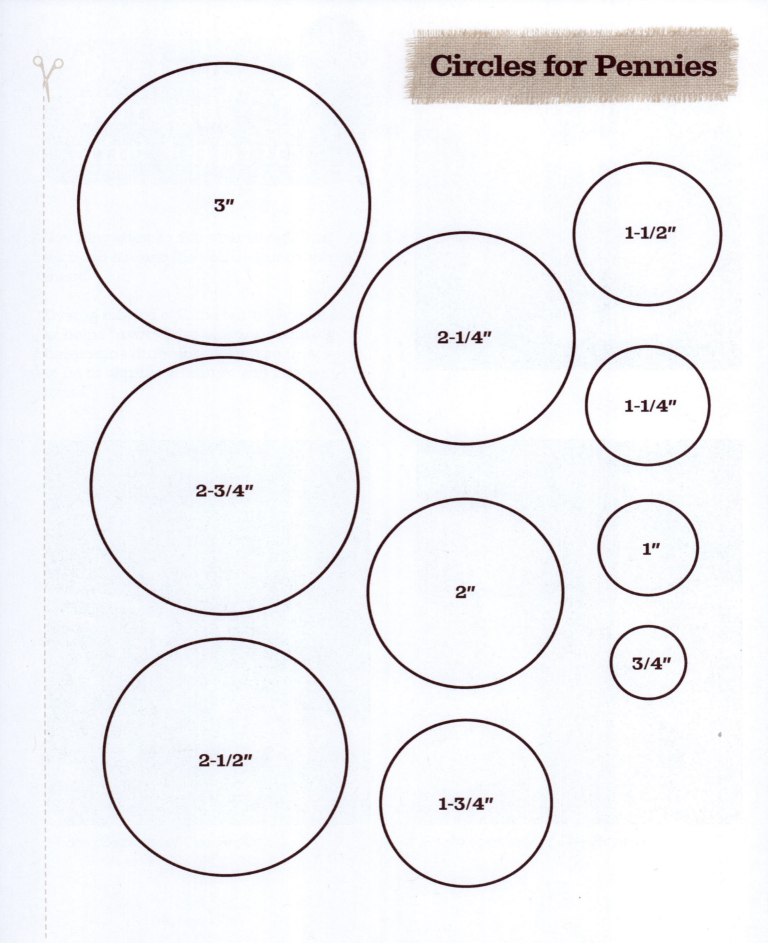

Penny Rugs and More: From the Beginning

Pinch Purse

Using large petal template:

- Cut three of outer fabric and three of inner (lining) fabric

Using small petal template:

- Cut three of batting
- Cut six lightweight plastic or cardboard for a firm liner (trim 3 petals by a scant 1/8")

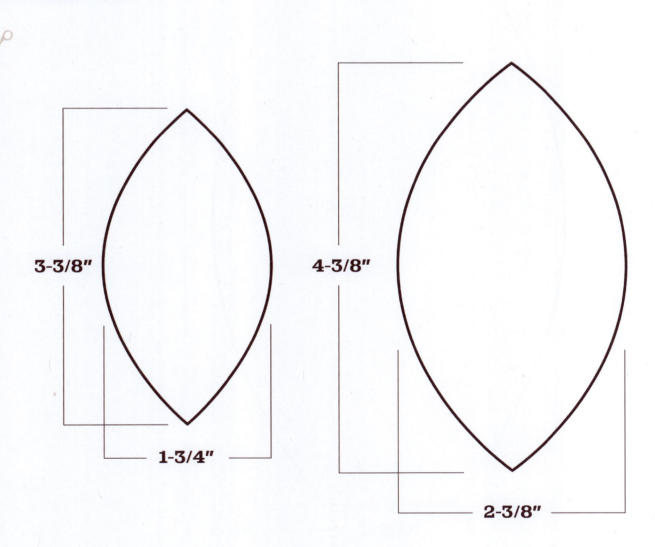

Make-Do Pincushion

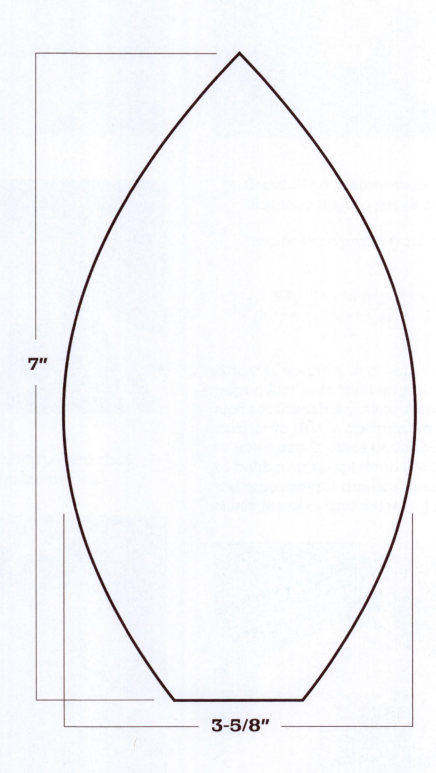

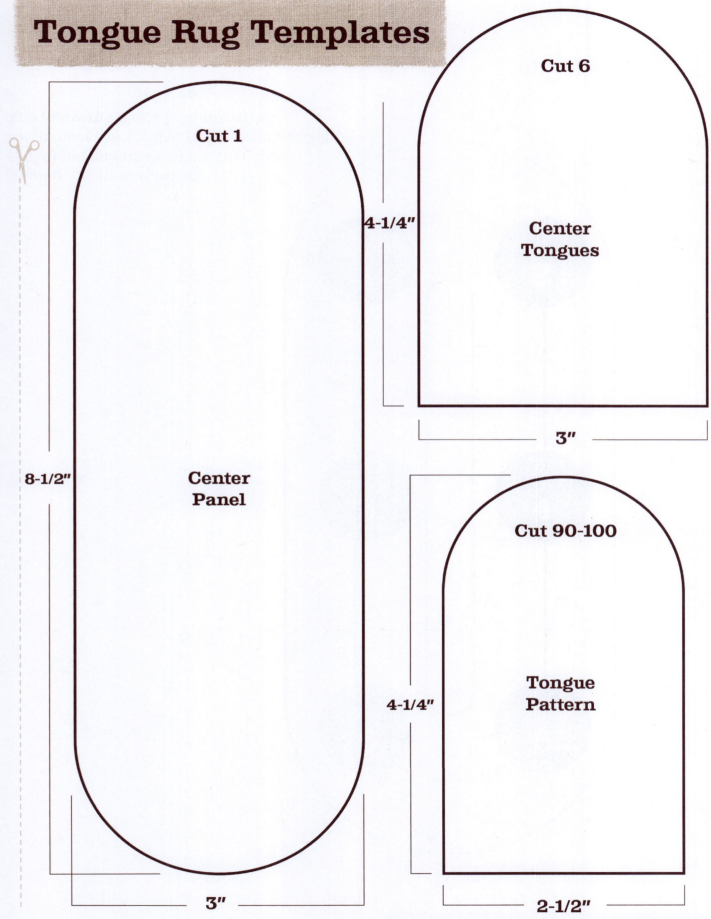

Tongue Rug Layout

The following pages contain all six sections of the Tongue Rug Layout template. Cut all dashed lines and match each section together as noted.

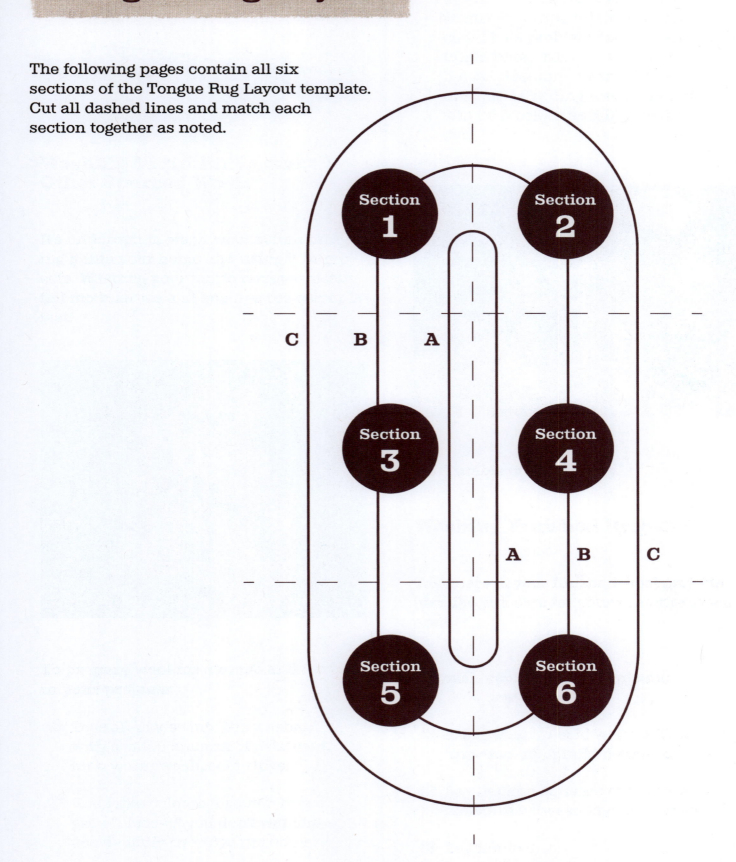

Penny Rugs and More: From the Beginning

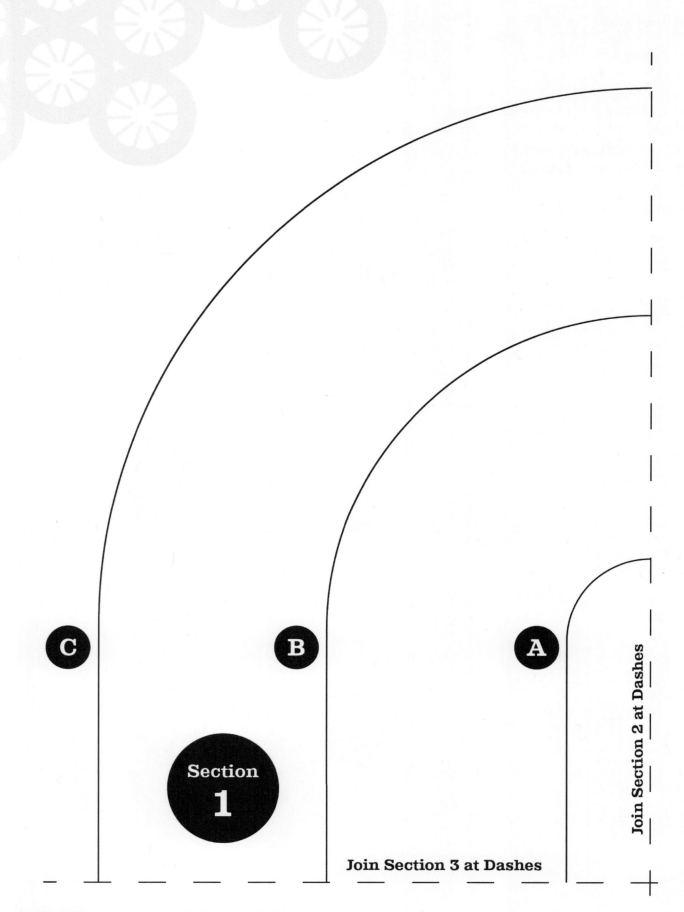

100 Penny Rugs and More: From the Beginning

Tongues overlap this way »

A

B

C

Join Section 1 at Dashes

Join Section 4 at Dashes

Section 2

Penny Rugs and More: From the Beginning ❀ 101

Join Section 1 at Dashes

Join Section 4 at Dashes

C

B

A

Section 3

Join Section 5 at Dashes

104 ❈ Penny Rugs and More: From the Beginning

Join Section 2 at Dashes

Join Section 3 at Dashes

A

B

C

Section 4

Join Section 6 at Dashes

Penny Rugs and More: From the Beginning ✳ 105

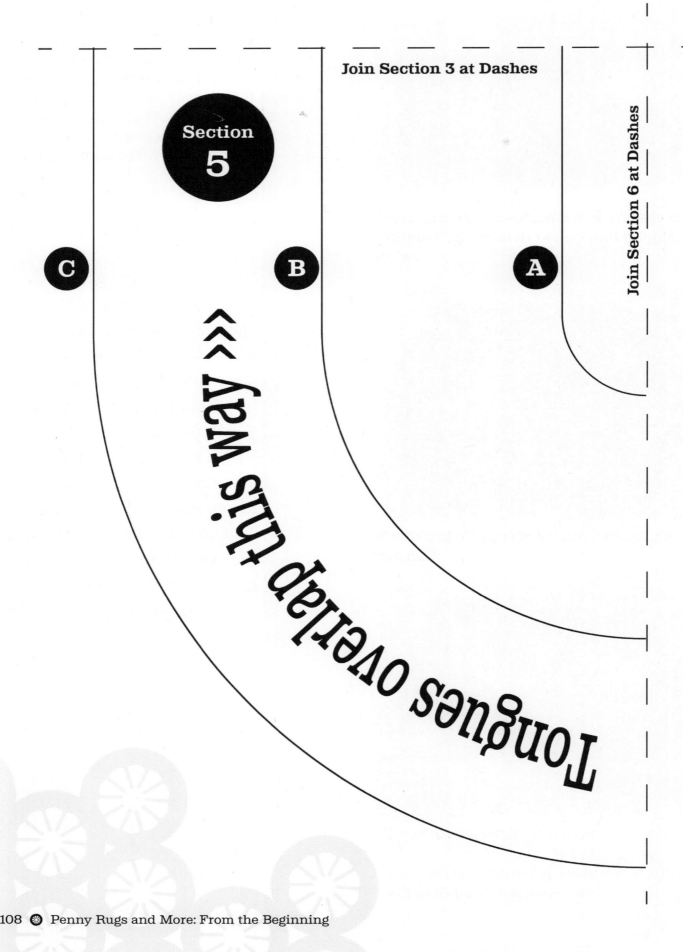

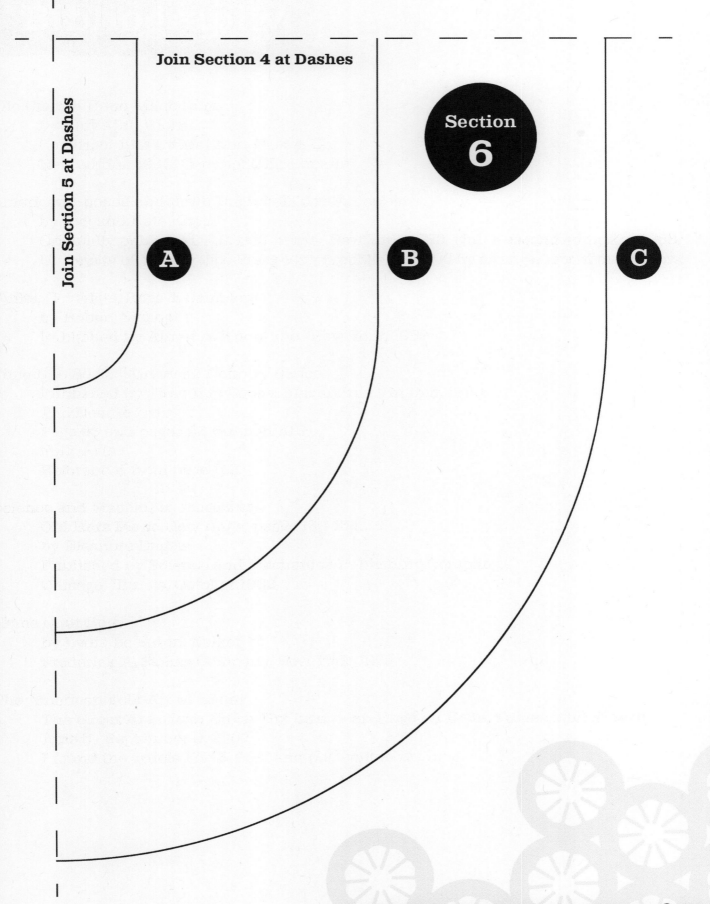

Bibliography

The Craft of Hand-Made Rugs
    by Amy Mali Hicks
    Copyright 1914 by McBride, Nast & Co.
    New edition 1936, Copyright, Friedmans'

American Hooked and Sewn Rugs, Folk Art Underfoot
    by Joel and Kate Kopp
    Originally published: E.P. Dutton Inc., New York, 1980, with a second edition in 1985.
    University of New Mexico Press edition published 1995 by arrangement of the authors.

Quilts, Coverlets, Rugs & Samplers
    by Robert Bishop
    Published by Alfred A. Knopf Inc., New York, 1982

Time-Life Books, American Country Series
    Published by Time-Life Books, Alexandria, Virginia, 1990
    The Needle Arts
    Page 93 and pages 96 through 101.
    Folk Arts
    References from page 142.

Science and Mechanics magazine
    Old Hats Make New Rugs, pages 130-134.
    by Eleanore Engels
    Published by Science and Mechanics Publishing Company,
    Chicago, Illinois, October 1952

Home Craft Rugs
    by Lydia Le Baron Walker
    Frederick A. Stokes Company, New York, 1929

The American Folk-Art Museum
    The Great American Cover Up: American Rugs on Beds, Tables, and Floors
    June 5 - September 9, 2007
    I found the article Feb 3, 2017 and posted it to my blog.
    https://folkartmuseum.org/exhibitions/the-great-cover-up-american-rugs-on-beds-tables-and-floors/

References

Better Homes and Gardens Traditional American Crafts

Country Living's Handmade Country

Early American Life Magazine

Back issues of Country Home and Country Living magazines

Clothes Moths: Fact Vs. Fiction
    By Kristine Kelly, September 23, 2018
    https://www.youtube.com/watch?v=-QLh0BFr0jo

Paula Burch's All About Hand Dyeing
    http://www.pburch.net/dyeing/FAQ/vinegar_for_dyeing.shtml
    http://www.pburch.net/dyeing.shtml
    By Paula E. Burch, Ph.D 19982022

*All photos are my own, except where noted.

Acknowledgements

All antique rug photos are credited to these lovely ladies:

April Leas, Kara Bowles, and M. Delores Tolley Sommers.
They source, collect, and save these precious antique mats and rugs.
Thank you, ladies, ever so much for letting me share your treasured rugs.

I would also like to especially thank my editor, Karen Rempel of New York, NY, for her patience and skills. And the very talented Doug McKinnon of Stride Graphics, Surrey, BC, Canada, for his expertise in photo enhancement, layout, and graphic design.

I am forever grateful to Cee Rafuse for her encouragement and guidance, otherwise I wouldn't have written this book. And when I needed photos of dyed wool, Cee came to my rescue!

Lastly, Jerome, thank you for all the care, kindness, patience, and love.

Afterword

I hope you've enjoyed this book and feel inspired to create your own heirloom penny rugs.

Colleen

Printed in Great Britain
by Amazon